The Ocean Between Us

"A Journey Through Distance, Memory, and Healing"

Eshna Verma

BookLeaf Publishing

India | USA | UK

Copyright © Eshna Verma
All Rights Reserved.

This book has been self-published with all reasonable efforts taken to make the material error-free by the author. No part of this book shall be used, reproduced in any manner whatsoever without written permission from the author, except in the case of brief quotations embodied in critical articles and reviews.

The Author of this book is solely responsible and liable for its content including but not limited to the views, representations, descriptions, statements, information, opinions, and references ["Content"]. The Content of this book shall not constitute or be construed or deemed to reflect the opinion or expression of the Publisher or Editor. Neither the Publisher nor Editor endorse or approve the Content of this book or guarantee the reliability, accuracy, or completeness of the Content published herein and do not make any representations or warranties of any kind, express or implied, including but not limited to the implied warranties of merchantability, fitness for a particular purpose.

The Publisher and Editor shall not be liable whatsoever...

Made with ❤ on the BookLeaf Publishing Platform
www.bookleafpub.in
www.bookleafpub.com

Dedication

To the ones who have shaped my heart,
To the quiet moments that taught me to heal,
And to the love that blooms when we least expect it—
This book is for you.

May you always find the strength to begin anew.

Preface

Admist life's chaos and noise, we often find ourselves lost in the search for healing, for love, for purpose. "The Ocean Between Us" is collection of poems and a reflection of the journey toward self-discovery and renewal. It is about how the heart, despite its struggles, has the ability to bloom again. It speaks to the beauty of new beginnings, the wisdom of self-love, and the deep-rooted power that lies within us all.

Each poem is a chapter of my own story, the moments of questioning, the reflections on what it means to truly heal, to truly love oneself, and to embrace the changes that life brings. These words are a celebration of growth, the silent strength that guides us through challenges, and the grace we discover when we learn to walk hand in hand with our own truth.

Through the process of writing, I've learned that endings aren't the final chapters, but rather the prelude to new and brighter beginnings. This collection, then, is not just mine—it is yours as well. It is a reminder that no matter where you are in your journey, there is always the possibility for renewal, for joy, and for finding peace within.

Acknowledgements

I extend my heartfelt gratitude to those who have walked beside me during the writing of this collection, both in life and in spirit. To my friends and family, thank you for your unwavering love and belief in me—your support was the quiet strength behind these words. To my parents and brother, you've shown me the power of language to heal and transform.

To my husband who arrived when the time was right— your presence has been my greatest gift.

To my readers, thank you for picking up this book and allowing these words to find a place in your heart. May you feel as much at home in these poems as I have in writing them. This journey is one we all share, and I hope these poems remind you that you are not alone. For you, this book is a testament to new beginnings, to love, and to the endless possibilities that lie ahead.

1. "The land of my Dream and Existence"

In the stillness of this moment,
I hear the echo of a time now distant,
When streets, though worn by age,
Were veins of life—alive with memory,
Where the rhythm of our youth beat steady
As we ran barefoot, innocent of tomorrow.

The colony—an empire in its own right—
Where every doorstep was a threshold to belonging,
And every neighbor more than kin.
Our shared existence was not one of mere proximity,
But a woven fabric of interlaced lives,
Each thread vibrant, intricate, inseparable.
The marketplace—an almanac of senses—
Its sounds, the pulse of a community,
Where the vendor's cry held the weight of tradition,
And fruits—golden and heavy—served as offerings,
A currency far more precious than gold.

We bartered in more than just goods,
But in trust, in moments of unspoken understanding.
I remember the soft murmur of my parents' names,
Whispered with a reverence that lingers still,
A respect born not from status,
But from the quiet strength of belonging,
From the roots they had planted in that soil,
From the way they had given more than they took.
And yet, time, that ceaseless tide,
Commands its own rhythm.

It carried us away—gently, but surely—
Like ships cast adrift on an ocean of necessity.
And with each mile, a part of me stayed behind,
Clinging to the memory of streets, of faces,
Of a childhood woven into the fabric of place.
The distance between us stretches wide now,
A gulf that is not simply physical,
But one of experiences, of lives diverging,
Of untold stories built on different soil.

Yet the weight of the past remains heavy on my chest,
A gravity pulling me back to where we began.
I am no longer the child I was,
Yet that child lives within me still,
A constant, an anchor.

For though the ocean may separate us—
The tides of love, the tides of belonging,
Is carved in the marrow of my bones,
An inheritance I carry with reverence—
The ocean between us is vast,
But its pull? Unyielding.

2. "The Day You Made Me New"

I once knew quiet mornings, soft and slow,
With dreams half-formed, and nowhere to go.
I lived in rhythms all my own,
A heart that wandered, yet alone.

But then you came—my tiny sun,
A cry, a breath, a life begun.
And in that instant, wild and true,
The world turned bright, and I turned too.

Your fingers curled around my thumb,
And every past regret went numb.
The pieces of me I thought were lost,
Found home in you, no matter the cost.

I traded sleep for lullabies,
Learned stars anew through baby eyes.

The simplest things became brand new—
A leaf, a laugh, the sky so blue.

You made me braver, made me kind,
Unlocked a light I couldn't find.
Your giggles are my favorite song,
You made me feel like I belong.

Now life is mess and sticky hands,
Crayon walls and big demands.
But oh, I relish every day,
In ways I never used to say.

So here we are, eight years along,
You've made me fierce, and soft, and strong.
I once was me, but now I see—
The best of me was born with *you* in me.

3. "Still Looking for You"

It's been twenty years, but still I wait,
For just one knock, one twist of fate.
A voice that laughed, a hand that led—
The best of me went when you fled.

You weren't just cousin, you were more,
A brother, guide—my heart's own core.
In every storm, you were the light,
The calm that turned my wrongs to right.
You knew my silence, read my eyes,
Could lift me up without disguise.

When life felt cruel, and I felt small,
You made me feel ten feet tall.
But time is crueler than we know,
It takes and never lets us go.
The day you left, the colors drained—
And joy has never felt the same.

I search for signs in stars and skies,

In strangers' words, in lullabies.
But no one speaks the way you did,
No one sees the soul I hid.
I stumble now, unguided, blind,
Still reaching for what's left behind.

The void you left, it yawns so wide,
No laugh, no hug can fill inside.
They say you're gone—I say you wait,
Beyond some softly glowing gate.
And I, with aching heart and eyes,
Just crave to meet you on *that* side.

Until that day, I live half-whole,
Still feeling you beneath my soul.
No matter how the years have curled—
You were my compass in this world.
And still, you are.

4. "The Sweetest Ache"

Loneliness came in soft at first,
A quiet hum, a gentle thirst.
A missing hand, an empty chair,
Just silence hanging in the air.

It didn't knock, it slipped inside,
And curled up where the tears would hide.
At first I fought, I begged, I screamed,
For noise, for touch—for what I'd dreamed.

But slowly, like the evening light,
It taught me how to love the night.
How shadows aren't so cold or cruel,
But deep and still, and strangely full.

I met myself in echoes deep,
In 3 AMs without much sleep.
No masks, no crowds, no games to play—
Just me, the truth, and what I'd say.

And something bloomed, so fierce, so real—
A kind of peace no crowd could steal.
No need to hide, no need to mend,
When you're your own beginning, end.

Now I drink silence like it's wine,
A bittersweet and sacred sign.
I crave the hush, the space, the void,
Where no one builds and none destroy.

It's strange—this ache, it feels like home,
A castle built when I'm alone.
And once you taste this quiet high,
No noise can thrill, no light can lie.

Addicted, yes—I won't pretend,
To loneliness, my ghost, my friend.
The world may dance and laugh and flee,
But nothing beats the depth of *me*.

5. "Where the Stars Remember Me"

There's something in the starry skies,
That speaks in hush, that never lies.
A shimmer soft, a silver thread,
That pulls me where the lost ones tread.

I lie beneath the velvet dome,
And feel more seen than here at home.
Each star, a whisper, old and wise,
A mirror floating in the skies.

The world below feels sharp and loud,
With heavy hearts and hurried crowds.
But up above, it's soft and wide—
No fear to fake, no pain to hide.

I've always felt a little torn,
Like I was borrowed, not quite born.
Like I belonged beyond this blue,
To realms where stars remember *you*.

Where voices hum in ancient light,
And dreams take form in endless night.
Where time is kind, and souls don't break,
And every wound becomes awake.

Maybe I'm stardust in disguise,
A cosmic echo in these eyes.
A stranger here, though I may seem—
But up there, love, I *am* the dream.

So when I gaze at skies so wide,
I feel my truth, I drop my pride.
And know this world is not the end—
The stars will call me home again.

6. "When I Wasn't Looking"

I wasn't searching, not that day,
Just passing time, just finding my way.
No stars aligned, no signs to see—
And yet, somehow... you found me.

No grand hello, no perfect line,
Just something quiet, pure, divine.
A glance, a laugh, the simplest start—
And suddenly, you had my heart.

You weren't a dream I dared to chase,
No perfect face, no fancy place.
But in your voice, I heard my name,
And knew I'd never be the same.

You fit me like a whispered prayer,
Like breath and soul were always there.
No need to try, no need to prove—
Just hearts that knew the way to move.

With you, love's not a dizzy fire,
But steady peace and calm desire.
A hand to hold, a soul to trust—
A kind of love that turns to *us*.

You are the still in all my wild,
The gentle hush, the inner child.
In your arms, the noise all ends—
The world softens, the spirit mends.

And now I know what poems meant,
What all those sleepless nights had sent.
You came not when I called above—
But when I *opened* to true love.

We are, in ways I can't define,
A sacred thread, a quiet sign.
Two hearts that knew, without a clue—
That I was made for love like you.

7. "The Last Place"

I love you in the quiet ways,
In stolen looks, in unseen days.
But love like mine, it doesn't shout—
It stays when all the lights burn out.

I held you in my secret chest,
The part of me I thought was best.
But you, you danced where crowds could see,
While slowly, you forgot *me*.

You live for now, for noise, for praise,
For faces bright and fleeting days.
And I? I live in silent nights,
In broken hopes and unseen fights.

You made me wait, you placed me last,
A shadow chained to all your past.
Your promises, like paper thin,
Would tear before they reached my skin.

I smiled through tears you never caught,
Fell quiet in the wars I fought.
And jealousy—my bitter friend—
Sat with me when you would pretend.

I watched you give the world your best,
While I became what's left, what's *less*.
You told me love, but lived a lie,
And left me asking always *why*.

And when I cracked, when I let go,
You whispered "sorry" soft and low.
But what is sorry to a wound,
That's bled so long, it's just a tomb?

Too late, too hollow, far too small—
A word can't catch a soul in fall.
You had my heart and looked away,
Now *sorry* has no place to stay.

8. "A Lifetime in a Day"

It wasn't just a date—we knew,
From how the sky turned deeper blue.
From how the hours slipped like sand,
While time just bowed to where we stand.

One coffee turned to stories deep,
We talked of dreams and fears we keep.
You smiled, and I forgot the rest—
The world, the weight upon my chest.

You laughed like home, like open skies,
With kindness glowing in your eyes.
And every word, and every glance—
Felt like I'd known you all by chance.

But chance, it seems, is love's disguise—
A plan unfolding in surprise.
We matched like verses in a song,
Like we'd been writing all along.

Your humor danced with mine so light,
A rhythm born of shared insight.
The jokes, the pauses, every cue—
You saw me clear, and I saw *you*.

And in those hours—small, complete—
I felt my heart regain its beat.
Not rushed, not wild, not some cliché,
But steady love that chose to *stay*.

You didn't try to impress or win—
You just let all the truth begin.
And I, with every word you gave,
Felt safe enough to just be brave.

Now I replay it in my mind,
That little day, that rarest find.
We didn't just go out—we *lived*,
In every glance, in all you give.

So here's my heart, in quiet thanks,
For how you filled in all the blanks.
For showing me what love could be—
When two souls meet, and just feel *free*.

9. "Back to the Lanes I Loved"

I left the town, but it lives in me,
In echoes of *budhiya kabaddi*,
In calls of laughter down the street,
Barefoot games in burning heat.

The *kaner* tree stood tall and wise,
Its pink blooms brushing open skies.
We'd sit beneath its quiet shade,
Trading secrets, plans we made.

The mangoes—oh, those mango days!
Sticky hands and golden haze.
We'd steal them green, we'd eat them ripe,
As if they held our childhood type.

Each house knew names, each gate was wide,
No locked-up hearts, no need to hide.
Colony friends like soul-born kin,
We lost the time, but not the grin.

Our chappals flung on dusty ground,
As laughter was the only sound.
We fought, we cried, we made amends,
Back then, we never lost our friends.

The mothers yelled, "Come home, it's late!"
But we'd sneak in through the broken gate.
A shared cold drink, a half-won race,
Each corner held a sacred place.

I still can hear our childhood song,
Those filmy tunes we'd hum along.
A broken radio, a terrace moon,
And hearts that wished they'd never swoon.

Some faces now have drifted far,
But shine inside, my brightest stars.
Their voices hum when I'm alone,
As if they're calling me back home.

The Diwalis lit with reckless sparks,
The cricket games in dusty parks.
The fights, the pacts, the secret codes—
That only lived in childhood modes.

And though I've walked a hundred ways,

Through city lights and grown-up days,
There's still a part of me that roams—
Back to those lanes, back to those homes.

I miss the love that didn't change,
Unfiltered, raw, a bit deranged.
Where no one judged, and all could be,
Exactly who they dared to see.

And so I close my eyes tonight,
To chase those stars, to feel that light.
To be that child, just for a while,
In that old town, where hearts still smile.

10. "My Little Brother, My Quiet Strength"

I still remember the day you came—
A tiny breath, a brand-new name.
The world stood still, then softly turned,
And in my heart, a new light burned.

You were the chaos, the sweetest sound,
The little feet that shook the ground.
I held your hand, you held my heart,
And life just bloomed in every part.

From scraped-up knees to stubborn cries,
To questions asked with wide-eyed whys—
You grew, and so did I, you see,
Your birth made *me* a better me.

And now I watch, in quiet awe,
The man you are, the grace, the raw.
You carry burdens, calm and still,
With strength I envy, quiet will.

You stand where I once used to guide,
Now you're the one who's by my side.
In moments when I broke, you stayed,
Without a word, just love displayed.

You take care of things, all grown, so wise,
And yet I still see that spark in your eyes—
That same young boy with dreams so tall,
Who once would trip, and then just fall.

We don't talk like we used to do,
But I feel your heart, and I hope you feel mine too.
Life has its pace, its pull, its race,
But nothing will ever take your place.

As your elder sister, let me say—
I'm proud of you every single day.
And even in silence, if you ever fall,
Know I will run through *any* wall.

You're not just my brother, you're my pride,
My memory's laughter, my heart's inside.
I'll always be here, through storm or shine,
Forever yours, and forever mine.

So go ahead, keep rising high—

But don't forget this watching eye.
That little girl who once held you tight,
Still loves you more than words can write.

11. "I Am the Dreamer"

I dream—
Not just in sleep, but wide awake,
In every breath, each risk I take.
While others walk with feet on ground,
I float where stardust can be found.

I've built a world inside my mind,
Where time bends soft, where hearts are kind.
A fairy tale I've made my own,
Where I'm the queen upon the throne.

The world may call me lost or wild,
But dreams have raised me since a child.
They taught me hope, they made me see,
That more than what *is*—is what could be.

I live in stories, wear their skin,
Play every part I find within.
A warrior, a poet, a spark in disguise—

A phoenix that refuses to die.

Life is my stage, and I, its flame,
With roles to shift, and none the same.
Each tear, each laugh, each word I write,
Is me becoming my own light.

And though the world may chase the real,
My dreams are what I truly feel.
They shape me strong, they pull me through,
They teach me love, they make me *true*.

So let them call me what they will,
I'll chase my stars, I'll climb that hill.
For in my dreams, I find my voice—
And in their arms, I make my choice.

To live, to love, to boldly be,
The dreamer who was born to *see*.
Not what is safe, or sure, or small—
But the magic meant to touch us all.

12. "Back to Bettiah, Back to Us"

Childhood lived in *Bettiah* breeze,
In *Mohanpur*'s old tamarind trees.
Where hearts were light, and days were slow,
And love was all we'd need to know.

Grandma's stories lit the night,
With demons, gods, and stars in flight.
We'd sit around, wide-eyed and still,
While her soft voice would always thrill.

She wove her tales with magic thread,
Of lands where angels gently tread.
Each story wrapped in love and spice,
Like bedtime served with warm boiled rice.

Grandpa, quiet, calm and wise,
With radio near ears and thoughtful eyes.

His world played out in crackling tunes,
He taught us patience, taught us grace,
In every pause, in every trace.

He'd hum along, a peaceful hum,
With fingers tapping on the drum
Of memory, of stories past—
Of lives that move, yet hold us fast.

And oh, the cousins—wild and free,
A tribe of mischief, just like me.
We ran like wind through endless lands,
With scraped-up knees and tangled hands.

Fights that lasted half a day,
Then vanished with a game to play.
We shared our sweets, our secret fears,
And grew together through the years.

We built our worlds from sticks and stones,
With thrones of pillows, dreams full-grown.
The nights we spent beneath one roof,
Where love was loud and always proof.
Now time has flown, we live apart,
But all of them still fill my heart.

That house, that time—it shaped my soul,

A gentle place that made me whole.
No sky too vast, no time too wide—
Can steal the home I hold inside.

In *Bettiah's* sun, in *Mohanpur's* rain,
I find my joy, my root, my name.
So here's to Grandma's endless lore,
To Grandpa's radio by the door.
To cousin-souls and days so sweet—
Where life and love were most complete.

13. "The Gentle Giant of Knowledge"

In halls of thought where silence speaks,
He walked among the ancient Greeks—
A mind ablaze with history's thread,
A thousand voices in his head.

Each date, each name, each storied land,
He held them gently in his hand.
Before the world could simply "search,"
He was the wisdom, he was the church.

Students came from far and wide,
To sit in awe, to swell with pride.
His words like rivers, deep and wide,
Carved valleys in the minds they'd guide.

A scholar, yes—but more than that,
He wore no crown, no scholar's hat.
Just quiet strength, a soul refined,

A giant with a tender mind.

And in his arms I first was laid,
He knew my thoughts before I made
A single sound, a cry, a word—
To him, my silence still was heard.

The same quick wit, the quiet fire,
The curious eyes that dared inquire—
We share the blood, the laugh, the gaze,
The thirst for truth that never sways.

He taught me not just dates and kings,
But how the heart in silence sings.
That knowledge wears a kinder face
When softened by a gentle grace.

And now he sits with silver hair,
A grandfather beyond compare—
Still teaching, though the books are toys,
And wisdom flows through whispered joys.

His legacy walks down the lane
In students' thoughts, in love, in name.
And I, who watched him shape the past,
Now watch him in this role, recast.

He is my hero, calm and wise,
With a dream-filled soul and twinkling eyes.
If I should grow to be half true,
I'll know my roots, and what they grew.

So here's to him—the mind, the guide,
The man with quiet, roaring pride.
A father, scholar, heart so wide—
I walk with him, and by his side.

14. "Her Reflection in Me"

They'd laugh and say, *"Is that your sis?"*
And I would scowl, not liking this.
She was *my* mother, full of grace,
Not someone I could dare replace.

Too beautiful, too young, too bright—
It never quite sat with me right.
Because I knew the deeper part,
The lioness with the velvet heart.

She wore the crown, not hand-me-down.
I knew her hands, not just her face,
The ones that built our little place.
They didn't see what I could see—
The fire she held, quietly.
She moved through life without a pause,
A silent storm with no applause.

She cooked, she healed, she mended tears,

She held the weight of all our cares.
The queen of rooms that smelled like love,
The spine we never thought enough.

A lullaby in human form,
A shelter safe, a harbor warm.
And when I fell, and still today,
It's *her* name that I first will say.

Her voice, a balm that finds my skin,
Her strength, the thread I carry in.
In every choice, in how I speak,
I hear her tone inside my cheek.

Though once I swore, *"I'm not like you,"*
Now mirrors show that it's not true.
Since marriage shaped me, motherhood too,
I see her soul in what I do.

In sleepless nights and meals half-eaten,
In small defeats, and love unbeaten.
The same soft fire behind my eyes,
The same old truths I used to fight.

She's not just near—she lives in me,
A mirrored, breathing legacy.
Her skin? Still soft, still oddly young,

As if time spoke another tongue.

And now I wish for just a trace
Of that same glow upon my face.
But more than looks, it's what she gave:
A heart that knows how to be brave.

A love that bends but never breaks—
The kind a quiet goddess makes.
So here's to her—my north, my ground,
In her, my truest self is found.

And every time I lose my way,
I see her in the light of day.
The queen, the guide, the soul I see—
Forever her... reflected in me.

15. "The Horizon's Call"

The horizon, always just out of reach,
A line where earth and sky both preach—
A whispered promise of what's unknown,
A place where dreams and daylight are sown.

I stared at it, a child in awe,
Hoping to catch what it might draw.
A secret world, a land untold—
It beckoned me, both young and bold.

I loved the orange, that fire in the sky,
As it kissed the world goodbye.
A color rich with warmth and grace,
That painted every dream I'd chase.

It sparked a fire within my soul,
A constant push to make me whole.
It whispered, *"Go, there's more to see,"*
And so I followed, endlessly.

I built my world behind that line,
A place where stars and thoughts align.
A realm where time would bend and break,
Where shadows danced and hearts could wake.

In the orange glow, I found my peace—
A quiet realm where doubts would cease.
And though the world around me spun,
The horizon promised I'd not run.

The curves and slopes beyond the gaze,
The mystery that filled my days—
It wasn't just the sight I sought,
But all the dreams it gently brought.

A place for thought, a place to fly,
Where reason ceased and I could try.
The edge of day, the start of night,
Where everything feels pure and bright.

I always wondered what lay there,
Beyond the orange, in open air.
Perhaps a future or a fate,
A place where dreams could truly wait.

But still, it called me every day,
A pull I could not turn away.

And in that pull, I found my wings,
In chasing what the horizon sings.

Now, when I stand and see it wide,
The horizon still pulls at my side.
Not just a line, but something more—
A promise of what's worth waiting for.

In every sunset, in every dawn,
It reminds me to keep moving on.
Because the world, though far and vast,
Is waiting for me to make it last.

16. "Old Friends, Deep in Heart"

We don't have the photos that others keep,
No endless selfies, no memories in heaps.
We don't mark our days with grand events,
But our bond's a flame, never spent.

No trips together, no big nights out,
Yet in silence, we never doubt.
The threads that tie us, woven so tight,
Invisible, but still full of light.

You know my family, and I know yours,
We've shared our lives, our closed doors.
Through every joy, through every tear,
Our hearts have stayed, always near.

Not by pictures, not by posts,
But by the moments that matter most.
The quiet talks, the fleeting calls,
The times we've picked each other up when we fall.

No grand gestures, no party plans,
Yet you understand me like no one can.
We've seen the world in different ways,
But our bond hasn't aged through the years or days.

We don't need to meet to still be whole,
Your voice echoes deep within my soul.
And though the years may come and go,
This quiet connection continues to grow.

When life feels heavy, when roads get tough,
You're always there, always enough.
Not in pictures, but in the way
You've stood beside me every day.

No need for proof, no need to show,
Our bond is in the places we go—
The stories shared, the laughter found,
In memories that still resound.

You've helped shape me into who I am,
More than a friend, more than a plan.
You've defined me in ways unseen,
Not by the places we've been.

The memories are deeper than any frame,

They live in my heart, they call my name.
Though no digital trace of us exists,
Each moment we shared, I can't resist.

We may not meet, we may not speak,
But in the silence, I know you seek
The same bond, the same quiet love,
The connection that's blessed from above.

So here's to us—old friends, always near,
In heart, in spirit, forever dear.
Not bound by time, nor fleeting fame,
But by the memories, by the name.

17. "The Art of Loving Me"

I learned to love the quiet first,
The moments when the world feels cursed.
When all the noise begins to fade,
And I am left in light and shade.

I learned to smile without the need,
To seek approval or to plead.
To trust the voice that calls my name—
And whispers softly, "You're not the same."

I learned to hold my flaws with pride,
To look them in the eye, not hide.
To see the cracks as paths to grow,
And let the healing winds still blow.

I learned to stand without the mask,
To put my heart out, no more task.
For loving me, through thick and thin,
Means accepting all that's deep within.

The mirror now reflects my truth,
A soul that's weathered storms of youth.
No longer chasing what is not,
No longer seeking what I've sought.

For in my hands, I've found my worth,
No need to search the outer earth.
I am the treasure, raw and pure,
A love that's steady, strong, and sure.

The days are mine to shape and mold,
To walk the path, both young and old.
I've learned to dance, though not so free,
Still, every step belongs to me.

I cherish moments, soft and loud,
And stand my ground, though not too proud.
For loving me is not a fight,
But knowing that I am my light.

So here I stand, a work of art,
A masterpiece, with every part.
With every scar, with every line,
I see the beauty that's divine.

Self-love is not a fleeting goal,
But the dance between the mind and soul.

In loving me, I've learned to see,
The strength of who I'm meant to be.

18. "Together, We Rise"

In your eyes, I found my spark,
A light to guide me through the dark.
With every word, with every glance,
You gave me courage, made me dance.

No longer bound by doubts or fears,
I found my strength when you were near.
With you, I know there's nothing I can't face—
For in your love, I've found my grace.

You've been the wind beneath my wings,
The voice that whispers, *"Do great things."*
When all the world seemed far away,
You helped me see the brighter day.

Through every setback, every fall,
You picked me up, you gave me hope,
Believed in me when I couldn't see—
A vision that was just for me.

Together, we've learned what it means to strive,
To make our dreams not just survive,
But to thrive and grow with steady hands,
To build a life, to make our plans.

You taught me more than just to dream—
You showed me how to chase the stream.
How to take each step, to make it count,
How to raise each goal, no matter how high the mount.

I'm stronger now, with you by my side,
With every challenge, with every stride.
Your belief in me, a steady fire,
That fuels my heart, that takes me higher.

In your love, I find my power—
You are my strength in every hour.
Together, we rise, together we stand,
A force unshaken, hand in hand.

Grateful for the days we've shared,
For all the love, for all you've cared.
I've learned to work, I've learned to see—
That together, we can always be.

With you, I know there's no defeat,
With you, my dreams feel complete.

Thank you for the faith you've given,
In you, my world is always driven.

19. "Echoes of Goodbye"

Goodbyes are never truly done,
Not when the heart still beats as one.
They're just the pause, the silent space,
Where distance fades, but love leaves trace.
For though we part, we never stray,
Your spirit lingers in my day.

You live within the air I breathe,
In all the things I can't conceive.
In every bite of food I taste,
I find your presence, slow and chaste.
The flavors we once shared in fun,

Now linger long after you're gone.
The recipes, the simple joys,
Of meals we cooked, of shared ploys,
Live on in the taste, in the scent,
In every meal, your love is spent.
The songs we sang, the words we knew,
They play again, as though brand new.

In quiet moments, soft and sweet,
I hear your voice, I feel your beat.
The melodies we'd hum and share,
Still echo softly through the air.
No need for time or setting sun,
For in these songs, we're still as one.

The lanes we walked, the paths we took,
Every step, every turn we shook,
Still guide my feet, though you are far,
Like footprints etched beneath the stars.
Your presence wraps around each street,
In every corner, in each beat.

You're there in every step I take,
In every turn, in every wake.
The habits that we once did trace,
Still live with me, in every place.
The way you smiled, the way you spoke,
The quiet strength, the gentle joke.

You are in each moment now,
In every smile, in every vow.
Goodbyes may come, but you remain,
A part of me, a sweet refrain.
Nothing truly fades or goes,

For love is deeper than time shows.

You live within my every part,
Still close, still warm, within my heart.
Goodbyes are not the final end,
For memories are where we mend.
And through the years, I'll always know,
You're with me, where love does grow.

20. "In the Twilight of My Days"

New Beginnings
You came to me like evening light,
When shadows stretched and day turned night.
I often wonder, *Where were you,*
Before the dawn, before I knew?
Why did you wait until the sky
Had painted shades of the goodbye?
Why not earlier, when I was young,
When I still danced and brightly sung?

I asked the stars, I asked the sea,
Why you arrived when you did for me.
Was there a reason, was there a plan,
For you to walk beside this woman?
I needed you before the rain,
Before the heartache, before the pain.
Why didn't you come when I was whole?
When hope still lived within my soul?

But as I look at all we've done,
The battles fought, the victories won,
I see the answer in your eyes—
You came to me when it was time.
For life is built not just on years,
But on the moments we hold dear.
And in the twilight of my days,
You helped me find a brighter way.

For in the evening of my life,
You came and cut through all the strife.
With every word, with every smile,
You made each day feel worth the while.
Perhaps it wasn't time before,
For me to find what you have stored.
But now I know, with every breath,
You were the gift beyond my depth.

So, no more questions, no more why—
I'll let the years just pass me by.
For you arrived, and now I see,
You came at just the time for me.
And though the past may hold its weight,
You are the love that feels like fate.
For in your heart, I found my start,
A brand new life, a brand new heart.

21. "The Art of Self-Healing"

I used to think that healing took
A map, a guide, a final look.
A road to travel, a task to do,
A moment where I'd start anew.
But healing's not a line or chart,
It's learning to embrace each part.

The scars, the tears, the broken ties,
The quiet strength that slowly flies.
I learned the art of mending slow,
Of letting go and letting grow.
Of standing still when all I craved
Was to keep moving, to be saved.

But in the silence, I found my grace,
A soft embrace, a slower pace.
For healing doesn't rush or race—
It blooms in time, it finds its place.
With every step, I learned to see
That happiness was always free.

Not in the past or future bright,
But in the present, in the light.
I found the beauty in each flaw,
The strength in all I never saw.
New beginnings whispered loud—
A life rebuilt, soft and proud.

The road ahead is wide and clear,
The weight of past no longer here.
I've learned to dance, I've learned to sing,
To find my joy in everything.
A happy life is what I choose,
A life where I no longer lose

The battle with the past I fought—
For in my heart, I've found what's sought.
Self-healing isn't a final prize,
But a journey seen through kinder eyes.
A gift that comes from deep within,
A new life found, a love to spin.

I walk with hope, I walk with light,
Embracing each new day, each night.
For in the art of healing true,
I've found a life that's born anew.

www.ingramcontent.com/pod-product-compliance
Lightning Source LLC
Chambersburg PA
CBHW071510130726

47997CB00006B/2480